Collins

Cherry Blossoms

Mathematics

UKG

FS3

SERIES EDITOR: RANI THIPPAVAZZULA

Student + Teacher			Teacher-only	
a animations	**ia** activities	**g** games	**lp** lesson plans	**tn** teacher's notes
ilt instructor-led tutorials	**w** worksheets	**v** videos	**w** worksheets	**ak** answer keys
	audio			

Preface

Cherry Blossoms provides graded, age-appropriate learning opportunities targeting holistic skill development for children in the age group of 3 years to 8 years. The series aligns with the vision outlined in the National Education Policy, 2020 for early years. It spreads across five levels, Nursery (Foundational Stage 1) to Class 2 (Foundational Stage 5). The books use a combination of hands-on activities, frequent recapitulation and child-friendly artwork to facilitate learning.

The series comprises **40 books** and spans **English**, **Maths**, **General Awareness**, and **Art and Craft**. The series comes bundled with a **workbook** for each subject and a book of **rhymes** and **stories** for Foundational Stage 1 to 3.

This series integrates the essence of **NIPUN Bharat** guidelines, which extensively deal with Foundational Literacy and Numeracy. The series aims to motivate learners to read independently, to improve their vocabulary, number sense and spatial understanding. The **Foundational Literacy and Numeracy (FLN)** skills include the skills for developing their critical thinking, logical reasoning and creative skills, as well as the skills to enhance their ability to express themselves both verbally and in writing.

Cherry Blossoms Teacher Support Materials include:

Teacher's Resource Books: Comprises stories, activity banks, classroom management and assessment guidelines

Multimedia eBook: Consists of animations, audio, video, slide shows, and interactive exercises

Print-ready Worksheets: Additional worksheets for practice and reinforcement, present in the digital support

Digital Flashcards: Flashcards with embedded sounds and animations for letter formation and letter-sound association

Animations and Songs: Animated stories and rhymes set to tune

Interactive Games: Interactivities to reinforce concepts in a fun and engaging manner

A note on the activity banks (included in the Teacher's Manuals)

The activity banks comprise hands-on activities that will help children develop the requisite skills to attain age-appropriate learning goals. In keeping with Howard Gardener's theory of multiple intelligences, the activity banks include options and variations that enable teachers to provide a planned cycle of experiences and opportunities, which foster each type of intelligence, to every child in their classrooms. The activity banks equip teachers to use the strengths of children as a means of complementing their less developed areas by valuing and nurturing the inherent abilities of the children.

Rani Thippavazzula, former Academic Director, Ravindra Bharathi Group is an eminent educationist with over two decades of experience in teaching, administration and curriculum design and development. As an Academic Advisor for chain schools pan India, she is proficient in developing learning products and is a specialist in Differentiated Instruction, Enterprise Education and Early Childhood Education.

Learning and Development During the Early Years

The early years are the most significant years for growth, development and learning. During this period, children need adequate opportunities for stimulating experiences as these favourably affect various learning abilities. Learning experiences, when chosen and planned properly, fuel the innate curiosity of children, and stimulate their thought processes.

The goal of learning during the early years is to enhance the all-round development of personality and to inculcate healthy attitudes, life skills and good values. Creative play, well thought-out games and developmentally appropriate activities help children develop the necessary skills to achieve these goals. The skills that children need to acquire can broadly be categorized as:

Motor:
Motor skills pertain not only to gross motor activities like walking and jumping but also include fine motor activities like the ability to hold a pencil and write. The development of motor skills is facilitated through several graded activities.

Personal, Social and Emotional:
Personal, social and emotional development, necessary for the overall personality development of children, is achieved using a combination of hands-on activities, role plays and thought-provoking stories and rhymes.

Linguistic:
The ability to listen, speak, read and write is critical to success in formal learning environments.

Mathematical:
The development of mathematical ideas and concepts is important at this stage since children will continue to build on this learning for most of their years of schooling.

Knowledge and Understanding of the World:
This is achieved through activities that enable children to explore their surroundings at home and in the school, and interact with the people that they see around them.

Health and Safety: The idea of health and safety is introduced through activities, stories and retelling of real-life experiences to encourage children to focus on health and well-being.

Creative:
Creative skills are developed through a host of activities involving art, craft, painting, roleplays, etc.

Logical and Rational Thinking:
Activities that involve simple puzzles, pattern-completion and visual discrimination help children to develop logical and rational thinking skills.

Contents

WALKTHROUGH

New concepts introduced through short rhymes, followed by practice pages for reinforcement

DANCING BUTTERFLIES

Sing.

One butterfly with nothing to do
Along came 1 more and now there are two.

Two little butterflies flying free.
Along came 1 more and now there are three.

Three little butterflies flying high and low
Along came 1 more and now there are four.

Four little butterflies touching the sky
Along came 1 more and now there are five.

Five little butterflies play in the garden,
Singing in the rain, dancing in the sun.

UP AND AWAY

Sing.

Five little birds learn to fly
Says mama bird,
'Flap your wings up high!'

Flap, flap, flap, flap, up and away
The first bird flies and says, 'Yay!
Now I will fly, be it night or day.'

Flap, flap, flap, flap, up and away
The second bird flies and says, 'Yay!
Now I will fly, be it night or day.'

Flap, flap, flap, flap, up and away
The third bird flies and says, 'Yay!
Now I will fly, be it night or day.'

Flap, flap, flap, flap, up and away
The fourth bird flies and says, 'Yay!
Now I will fly, be it night or day.'

Flap, flap, flap, flap, up and away
The fifth bird flies and says, 'Yay!
Now I will fly, be it night or day.'

Counting beyond 10 continued using groups of 10

I CAN COUNT BY MAKING GROUPS OF 10

Colour the beads to make the given number.

11 and
16 and
12 and
17 and
13 and
18 and
14 and
15 and

Draw 1 more object. Count and write the total number.

Exercises to lay the foundation for number operations, which are introduced in the book

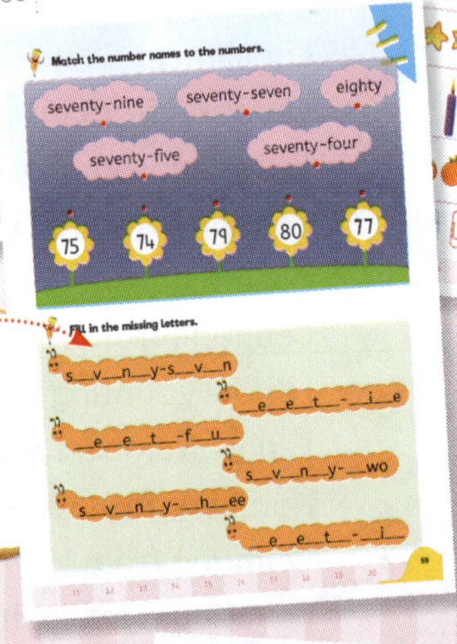

Match the number names to the numbers.

seventy-nine
seventy-seven
eighty
seventy-five
seventy-four

75 74 79 80 77

Fill in the missing letters.

Exercises in interesting formats to learn number names

Number bonds introduced as a precursor to the concepts of addition and subtraction

NUMBER BONDS

Draw the correct number of red dots. One has been done for you.

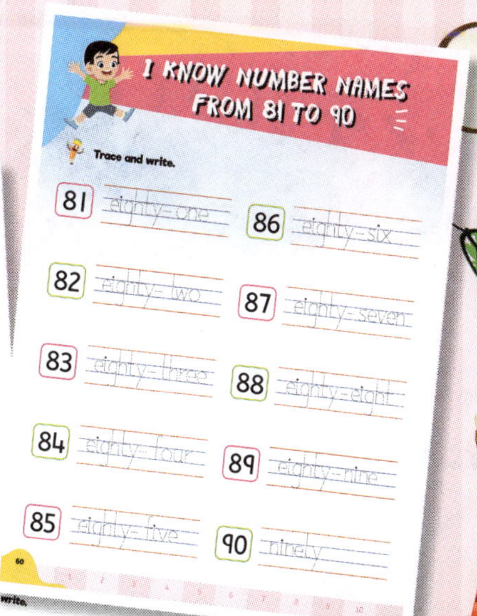

Frequent revision pages in various formats for recapitulation and reinforcement

Multiple opportunities for revision of rote counting

I KNOW!

Draw a big box.

small

big

Colour the thick pencil.

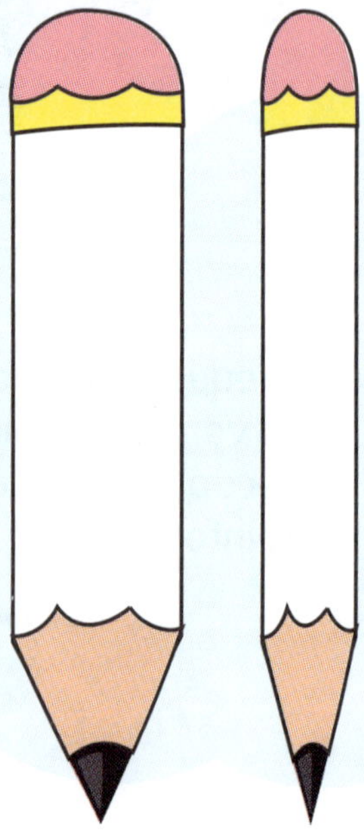

Cross out (✗) the short ladder.

Draw a fat snowman.

Draw an apple near the boy.

Ring the different object.

Cross out (✗) the empty vase.

Colour the animal with the long neck.

11 12 13 14 15 16 17 18 19 20

TALL, TALLER, TALLEST

Point and read.

Tick (✓) the tallest building.

1 2 3 4 5 6 7 8 9 10

Colour the tall lamp ●-orange, taller lamp ●-blue and tallest lamp ●-green.

Write 1 for the tallest ladder, 2 for the taller ladder and 3 for the tall ladder.

SHORT, SHORTER, SHORTEST

Point and read.

short shorter shortest

Tick (✓) the shortest cake.

Colour the short pencil ●-blue, shorter pencil ●-red and shortest pencil ●-yellow.

Write 1 for the shortest table, 2 for the shorter table and 3 for the short table.

HEAVY, HEAVIER, HEAVIEST

Point and read.

heavy heavier heaviest

Tick (✓) the heaviest fruit.

Colour the heaviest ●-grey, heavier ●-blue and heavy ●-black.

Write 1 for the heaviest lamb, 2 for the heavier lamb and 3 for the heavy lamb.

THIN, THINNER, THINNEST

Point and read.

Tick (✓) the thinnest candle.

Colour the thin candy ●-pink, thinner candy ●-red and thinnest candy ●-green.

thin   thinner   thinnest

Write 1 for the thinnest book, 2 for the thinner book and 3 for the thin book.

BIG, BIGGER, BIGGEST

Point and read.

big bigger biggest

Tick (✓) the biggest bear.

Colour the biggest glass ●-red, bigger glass ●-blue and big glass ●-green.

Write 1 for the biggest apple, 2 for the bigger apple and 3 for the big apple.

SMALL, SMALLER, SMALLEST

Point and read.

Tick (✓) the smallest circle.

Colour the small flower ●-red, smaller flower ●-yellow and smallest flower ●-pink.

Write 1 for the smallest cap, 2 for the smaller cap and 3 for the small cap.

I KNOW!

Ring the heavier pumpkin.

Ring the shortest lamppost.

Colour the biggest bee.

Colour the smallest ball.

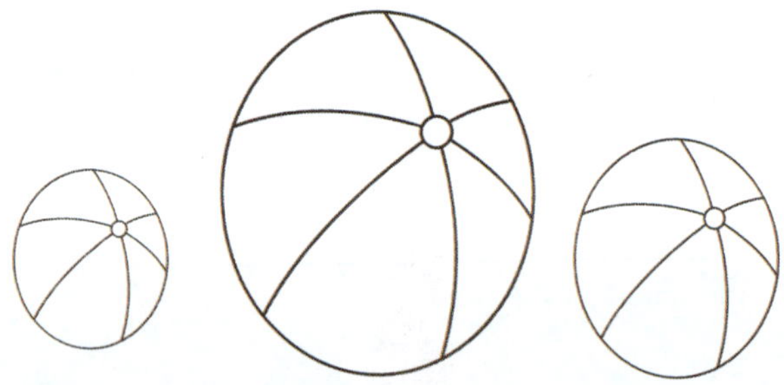

Tick (✓) the thinnest pencil.

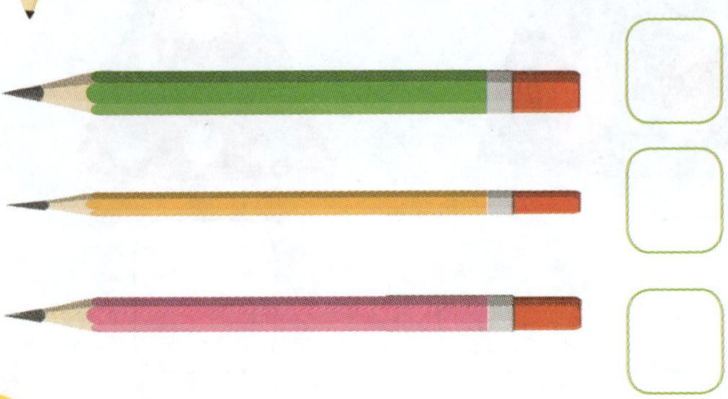

Tick (✓) the tallest candle.

UP AND AWAY

Sing.

Five little birds learn to fly
Says mama bird,
'Flap your wings up high!'

Flap, flap, flap, flap, up and away
The first bird flies and says, 'Yay!
Now I will fly, be it night or day.'

Flap, flap, flap, flap, up and away
The second bird flies and says, 'Yay!
Now I will fly, be it night or day.'

Flap, flap, flap, flap, up and away
The third bird flies and says, 'Yay!
Now I will fly, be it night or day.'

Flap, flap, flap, flap, up and away
The fourth bird flies and says, 'Yay!
Now I will fly, be it night or day.'

Flap, flap, flap, flap, up and away
The fifth bird flies and says, 'Yay!
Now I will fly, be it night or day.'

ORDINAL NUMBERS

Look at the picture. Point and read.

Match the child to the position.

fifth   fourth   third   second   first

Ring the second fruit. Count from the left.

Colour the fifth glass. Count from the left.

Draw a cup near the third bear. Count from the left.

Cross out (✗) the fourth toy. Count from the left.

I KNOW NUMBERS FROM 1 to 20

Match the pictures to the correct numbers.

1

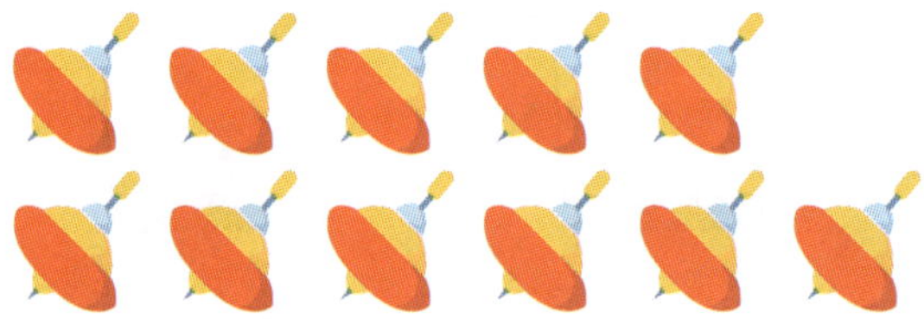

19

11

9

3

1 2 3 4 5 6 7 8 9 10

Colour the correct number of objects.

15

7

4

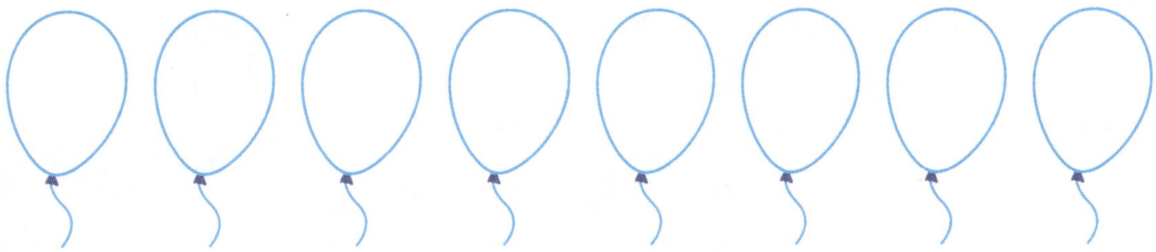

Skip count by 2's. Colour the correct boxes in red. One has been done for you.

1	2	3	4	5
6	7	8	9	10
11	12	13	14	15
16	17	18	19	20

I KNOW COUNTING FROM 1 to 50

Trace and write.

1	11	21	31	41
2	12	22	32	42
3	13	23	33	43
4	14	24	34	44
5	15	25	35	45
6	16	26	36	46
7	17	27	37	47
8	18	28	38	48
9	19	29	39	49
10	20	30	40	50

1 2 3 4 5 6 7 8 9 10

Colour the number that comes before.

Cross out (✗) the number that comes after.

Ring the number that comes in between.

I CAN COUNT BY MAKING GROUPS OF 10

Colour the beads to make the given number.

11 and

16 and

12 and

17 and

13 and

18 and

14 and

19 and

15 and

20 and

I KNOW NUMBERS NAMES FROM 1 to 20

Match the number to the correct number name.

1	two
2	seven
3	nine
4	one
5	eight
6	six
7	three
8	five
9	ten
10	four

Match the number to the correct number name.

11	twelve
12	seventeen
13	nineteen
14	eleven
15	eighteen
16	sixteen
17	thirteen
18	fifteen
19	twenty
20	fourteen

Fill in the blanks to complete the number names.

1. o _ e
2. t _ o
3. t _ r _ _
4. f _ _ r
5. f _ v _
6. s _ _
7. s _ _ en
8. e _ _ _ t
9. n _ _ _
10. _ _ n
11. el _ _ _ n
12. t _ _ l _ _
13. t _ _ rteen
14. f _ _ r _ _ _ n
15. f _ _ t _ _ n
16. _ ix _ _ _ _
17. se _ _ n _ _ _ _
18. _ igh _ _ _ _
19. n _ n _ _ een
20. t _ _ n _ _

I KNOW SHAPES

Trace and colour the circle.

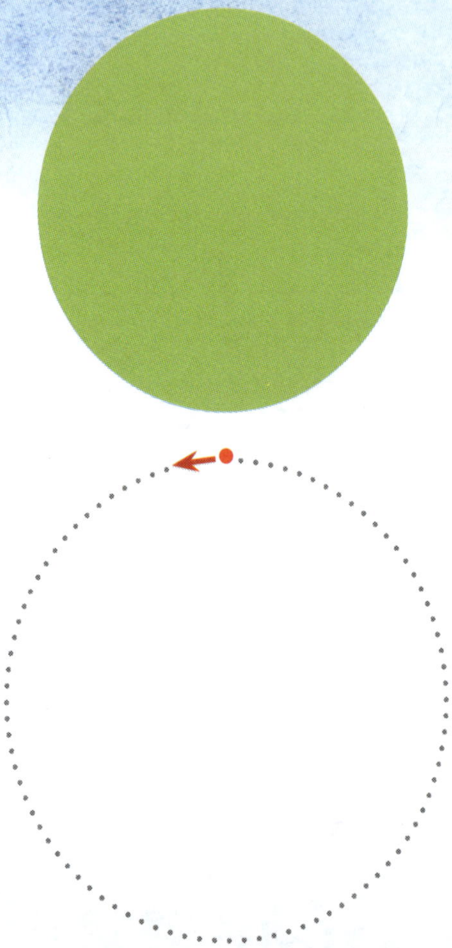

Trace and colour the star.

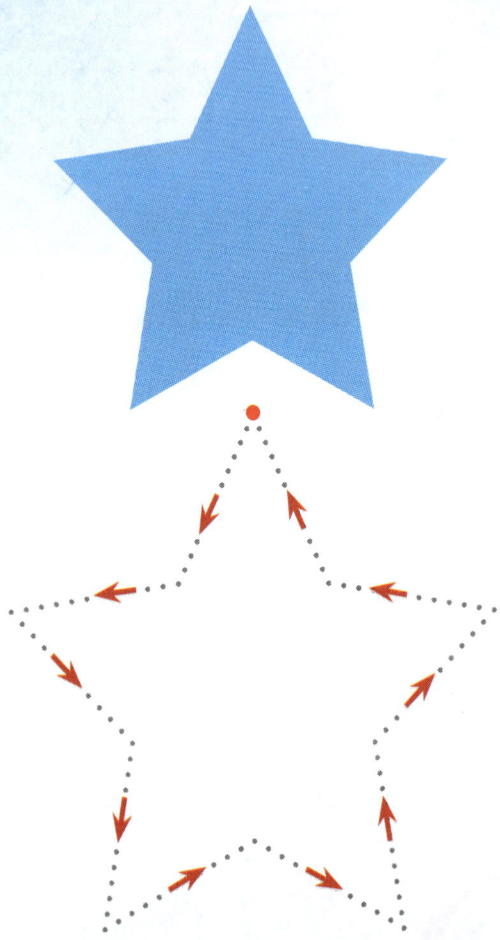

Trace and colour the semicircle.

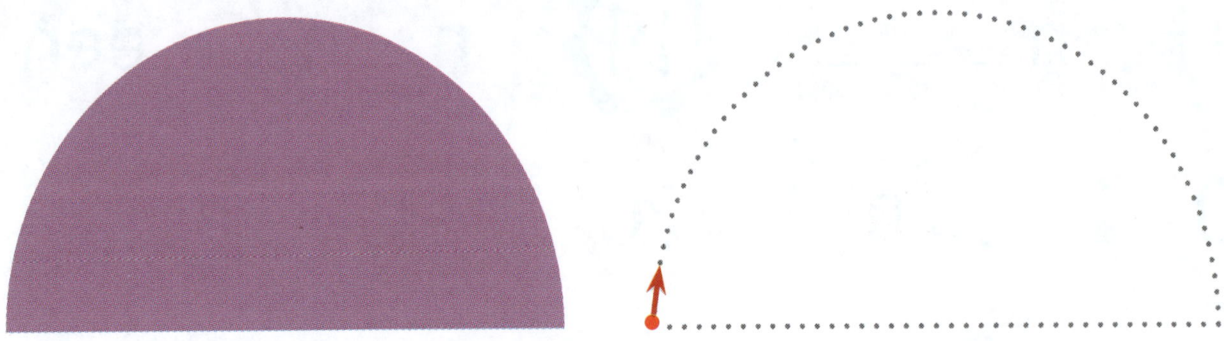

Cross (X) the odd one out.

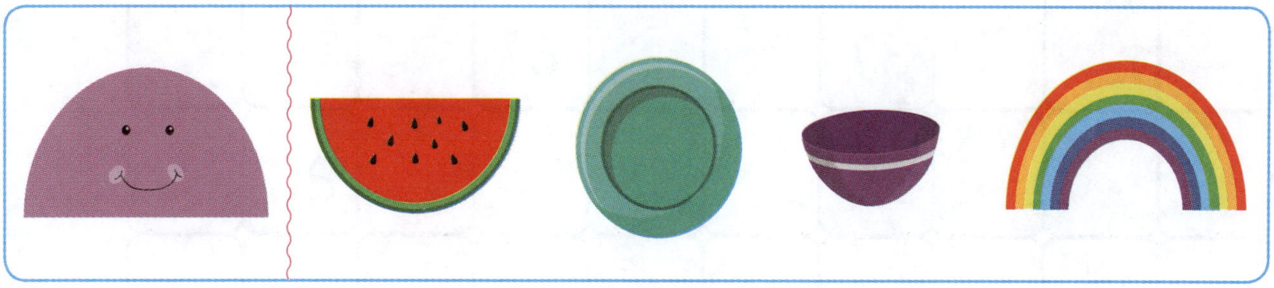

I KNOW COUNTING FROM 1 TO 100

Fill in the missing numbers.

1	11		31				71		
					52				92
			33					83	
	14			44		64			
		25							95
6							76		
			37			67			
					58			88	
	19			49					
		30							100

I KNOW NUMBERS FROM 51 TO 100

Match the pictures to the correct numbers.

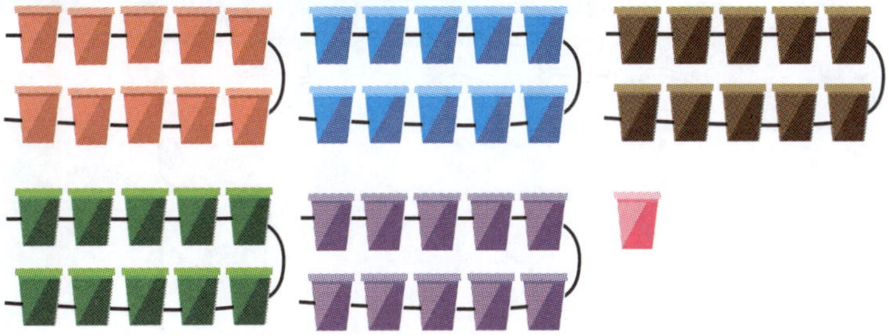

69

90

51

Colour the correct number of objects.

78

63

Skip count by 2's. Colour the correct boxes in red.
One has been done for you.

51	52	53	54	55
56	57	58	59	60
61	62	63	64	65
66	67	68	69	70

Write the numbers that come just before.

___ 63   ___ 92   ___ 76   ___ 84

Write the numbers that come just after.

81 ___   75 ___   98 ___   66 ___

Write the missing number between the given numbers.

54 ___ 56

82 ___ 84

68 ___ 70

79 ___ 81

NUMBERS TILL 100: MORE – LESS

Cross out (✗) the one that is more.

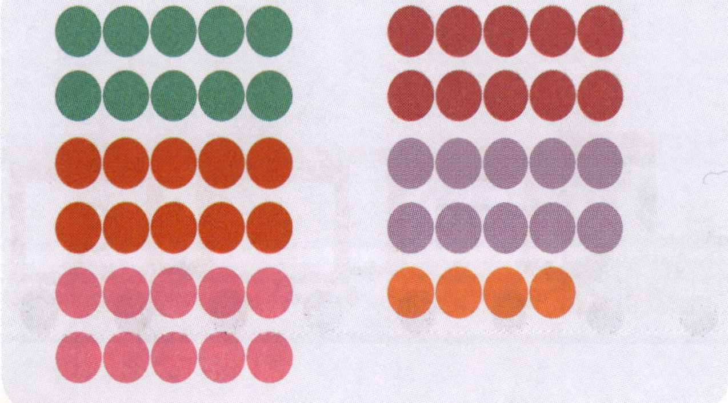

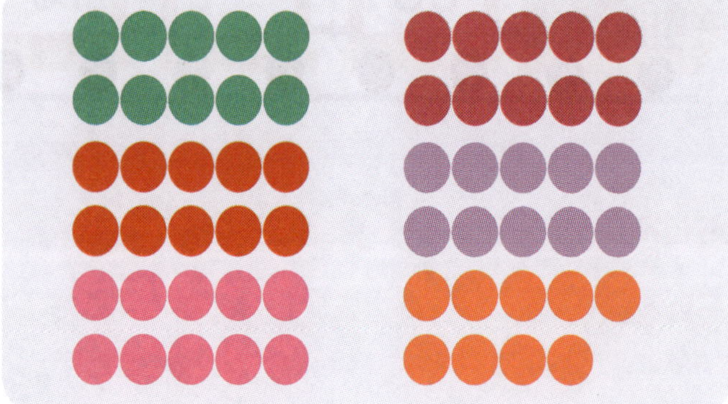

REVISION OF GROUPS OF 10

Match the number to the correct value.

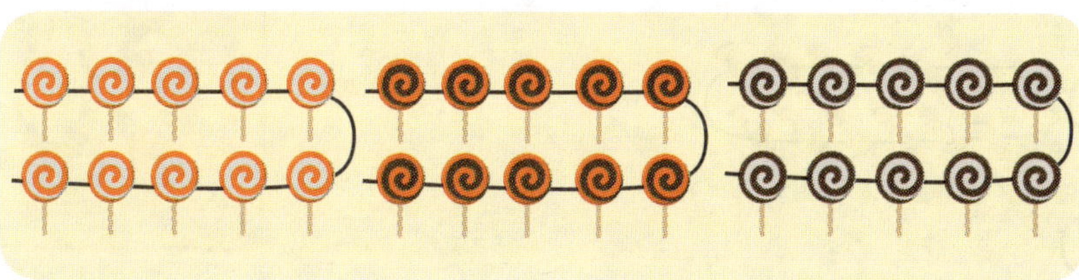

10

20

30

40

50

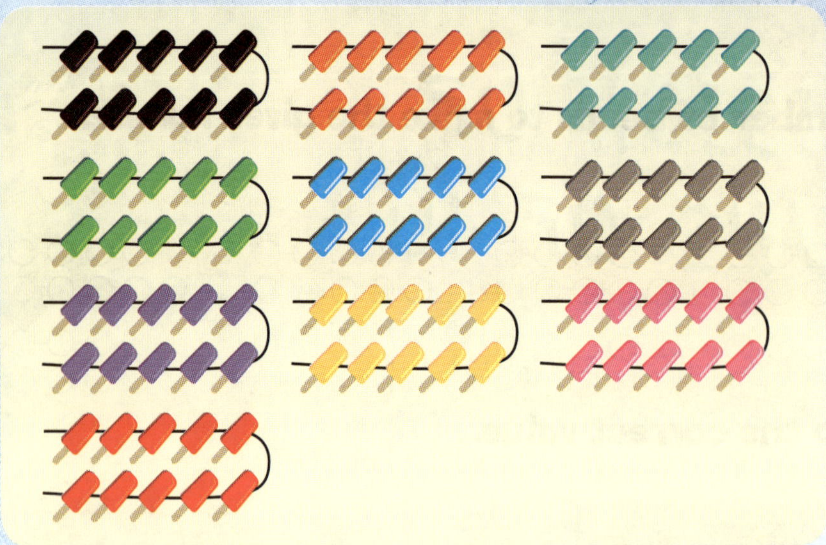

60

70

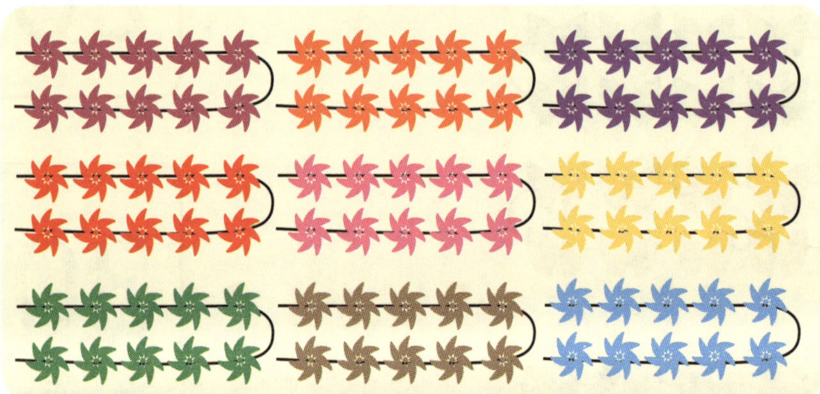

80

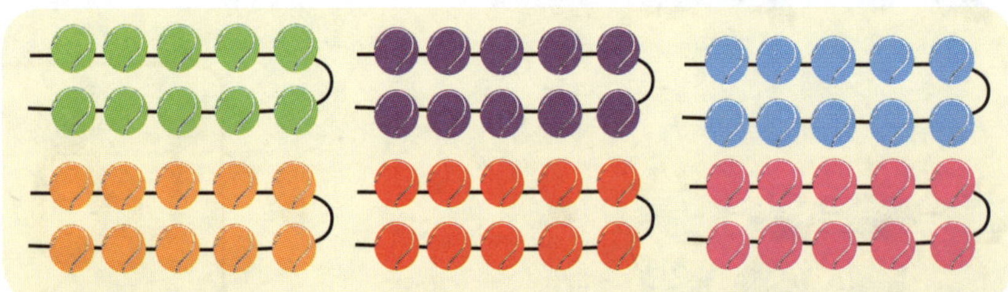

90

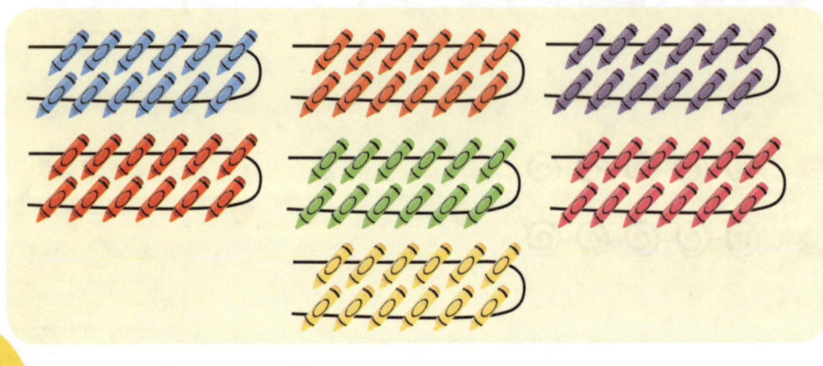

100

Colour the correct number of beads to make the given number.

91

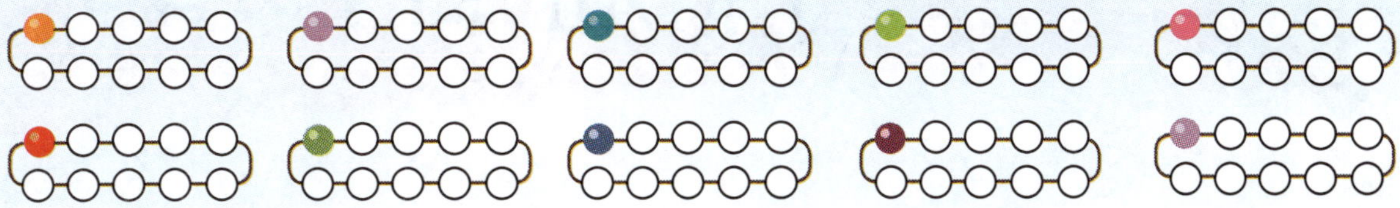

93

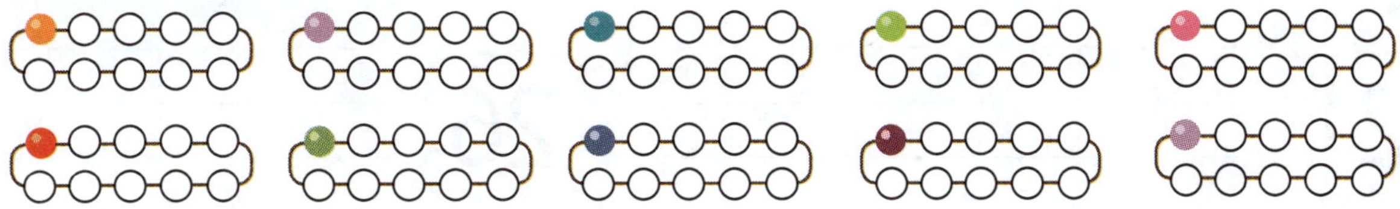

95

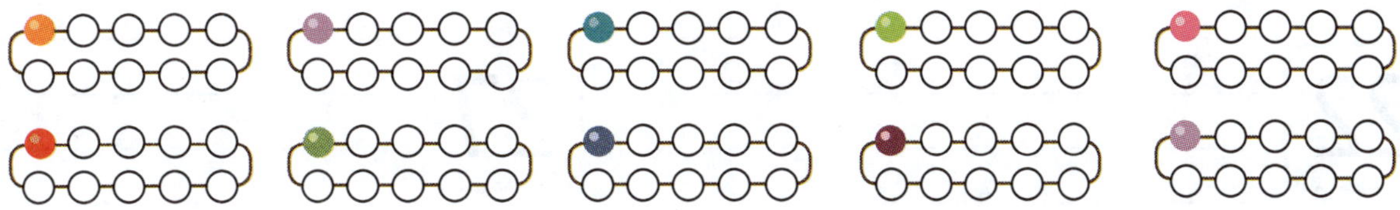

96

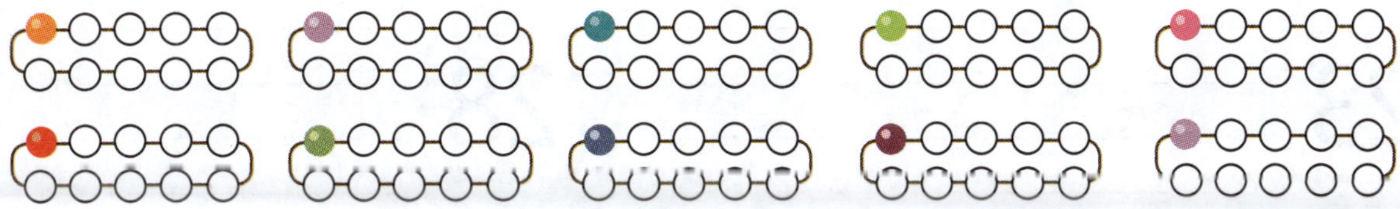

98

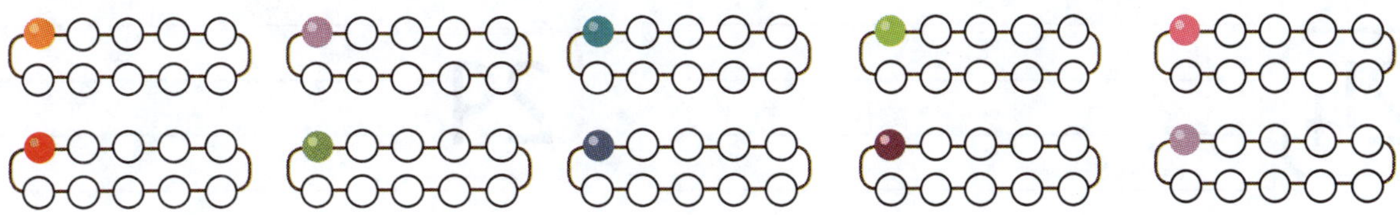

100

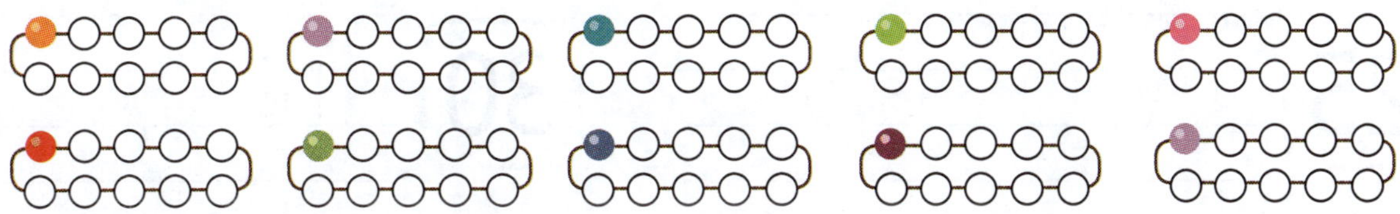

I KNOW NUMBER NAMES FROM 21 TO 30

Trace and write.

21	twenty-one	26	twenty-six
22	twenty-two	27	twenty-seven
23	twenty-three	28	twenty-eight
24	twenty-four	29	twenty-nine
25	twenty-five	30	thirty

Match the number names to the numbers.

twenty-one

thirty

twenty-three

twenty-eight

twenty-five

30 25 28 23 21

Fill in the missing letters.

t__e__t__-__wo

__we__t__-__h__ee

__we__t__-__ __x

t__e__t__-s__v__n

t__e__t__-__i__e

__we__t__-__i__ht

11 12 13 14 15 16 17 18 19 20

I KNOW NUMBER NAMES FROM 31 TO 40

Trace and write.

31 thirty-one

32 thirty-two

33 thirty-three

34 thirty-four

35 thirty-five

36 thirty-six

37 thirty-seven

38 thirty-eight

39 thirty-nine

40 forty

Match the number names to the numbers.

thirty-nine thirty-seven forty

thirty-five thirty-four

35 34 39 40 37

Fill in the missing letters.

t___i___t___-s___v___n

___h___r___y-___i___e

___h___r___y-f___u___

t___i___t___-___wo

t___i___t___-___h___ee

___h___r___y-___i___

I KNOW NUMBER NAMES FROM 41 TO 50

Trace and write.

41 forty-one

46 forty-six

42 forty-two

47 forty-seven

43 forty-three

48 forty-eight

44 forty-four

49 forty-nine

45 forty-five

50 fifty

Match the number names to the numbers.

fifty

forty-one

forty-three

forty-eight

forty-five

41 45 43 48 50

Fill in the missing letters.

f__r__y-__wo

__o__t__-__h__ee

__o__t__-__ __x

f__r__y-s__v__n

f__r__y-__i__e

__o__t__-__i__ht

3D SHAPES

Colour the objects in each row that match the shape given.

Sphere

Cone

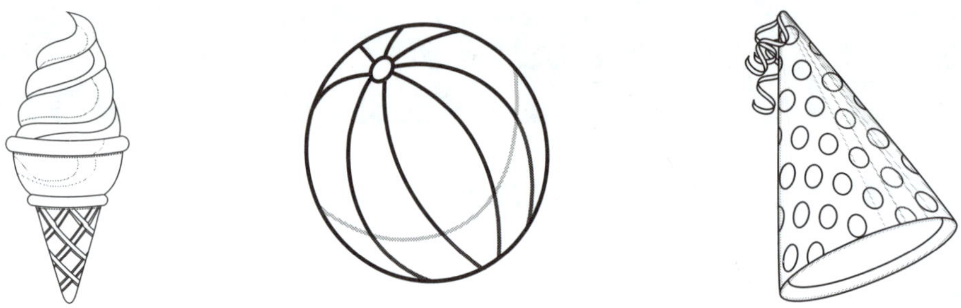

Cylinder

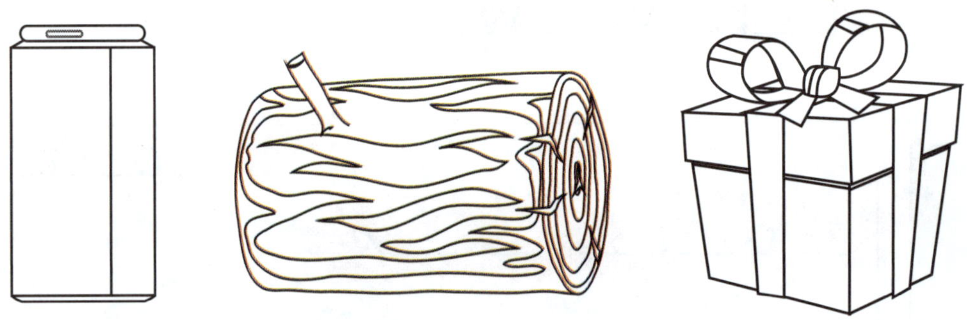

Cube

Paste stickers of 3D objects that match the given shape.

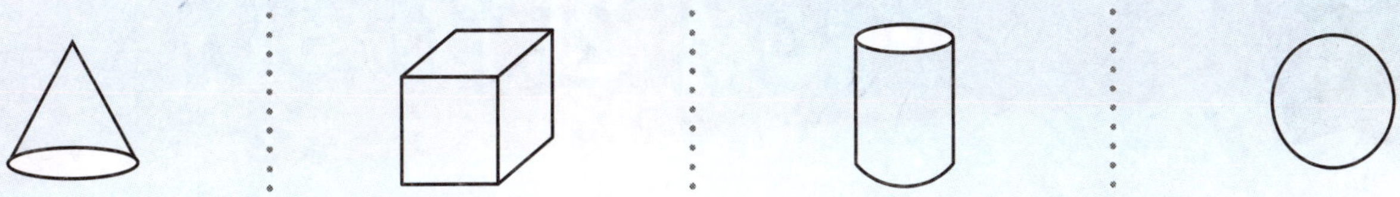

How many shapes do you see?

 =

 =

 =

 =

I KNOW NUMBER NAMES FROM 21 TO 50

Match the number to the correct number name.

23	• •	thirty
26	• •	twenty-seven
21	• •	twenty-nine
24	• •	twenty-one
25	• •	twenty-eight
22	• •	twenty-two
27	• •	twenty-three
30	• •	twenty-five
29	• •	twenty-six
28	• •	twenty-four

Match the number to the correct number name.

31		forty-two
42		fifty
33		forty-nine
44		thirty-one
35		thirty-eight
36		thirty-six
47		thirty-three
38		thirty-five
49		forty-seven
50		forty-four

I KNOW NUMBER NAMES FROM 51 TO 60

Trace and write.

51	fifty-one	56	fifty-six
52	fifty-two	57	fifty-seven
53	fifty-three	58	fifty-eight
54	fifty-four	59	fifty-nine
55	fifty-five	60	sixty

Match the number names to the numbers.

fifty-nine

sixty

fifty-seven

fifty-five

fifty-four

55 54 59 60 57

Fill in the missing letters.

f__f__y-s__v__n

__i__t__-__i__e

__i__t__-f__u__

f__f__y-__wo

f__f__y-__h__ee

__i__t__-__i__

I KNOW NUMBER NAMES FROM 61 TO 70

Trace and write.

61	sixty-one	66	sixty-six
62	sixty-two	67	sixty-seven
63	sixty-three	68	sixty-eight
64	sixty-four	69	sixty-nine
65	sixty-five	70	seventy

Match the number names to the numbers.

seventy   sixty-one   sixty-three

sixty-eight   sixty-five

61   65   63   68   70

Fill in the missing letters.

s___x___y-___wo

___i___t___-___h___ee

___i___t___-___ ___x

s___x___y-s___v___n

s___x___y-___i___e

___i___t___-___i___ht

I KNOW NUMBER NAMES FROM 71 TO 80

Trace and write.

71 seventy-one

76 seventy-six

72 seventy-two

77 seventy-seven

73 seventy-three

78 seventy-eight

74 seventy-four

79 seventy-nine

75 seventy-five

80 eighty

Match the number names to the numbers.

seventy-nine | seventy-seven | eighty

seventy-five | seventy-four

75 | 74 | 79 | 80 | 77

Fill in the missing letters.

s__v__n__y-s__v__n

__e__e__t__-__i__e

__e__e__t__-f__u__

s__v__n__y-__wo

s__v__n__y-__h__ee

__e__e__t__-__i__

I KNOW NUMBER NAMES FROM 81 TO 90

Trace and write.

81	eighty-one	86	eighty-six
82	eighty-two	87	eighty-seven
83	eighty-three	88	eighty-eight
84	eighty-four	89	eighty-nine
85	eighty-five	90	ninety

Match the number names to the numbers.

ninety

eighty-one

eighty-three

eighty-eight

eighty-five

81 85 83 88 90

Fill in the missing letters.

e__g__t__-__wo

__i__h__y-__h__ee

__i__h__y-__ __x

e__g__t__-s__v__n

e__g__t__-__i__e

__i__h__y-__i__ht

I KNOW NUMBER NAMES FROM 91 TO 100

Trace and write.

91 ninety-one	96 ninety-six
92 ninety-two	97 ninety-seven
93 ninety-three	98 ninety-eight
94 ninety-four	99 ninety-nine
95 ninety-five	100 hundred

Match the number names to the numbers.

ninety-nine   ninety-seven   hundred

ninety-five   ninety-four

95   94   99   100   97

Fill in the missing letters.

n__n__t__-s__v__n

__i__e__y-__i__e

__i__e__y-f__u__

n__n__t__-__wo

n__n__t__-__h__ee

__i__e__y-__i__

I KNOW NUMBER NAMES FROM 51 TO 100

Match the number to the correct number name.

74	fifty-nine
52	sixty-three
53	sixty-eight
78	seventy-four
71	fifty-eight
56	fifty-two
63	fifty-three
58	seventy-one
59	fifty-six
68	seventy-eight

Match the number to the correct number name.

73	seventy-six
64	fifty-four
61	sixty-nine
72	sixty-one
65	seventy-two
76	eighty
54	seventy-three
66	sixty-five
69	sixty-six
80	sixty-four

11 12 13 14 15 16 17 18 19 20

SKIP COUNTING BY 2'S

Look at the picture. Trace the path of the butterfly.

1 2 3 4 5 6 7 8 9 10 11 12 13 14 15

Colour every second number. One has been done for you.

1	2	3	4	5	6	7	8	9	10
11	12	13	14	15	16	17	18	19	20
21	22	23	24	25	26	27	28	29	30
31	32	33	34	35	36	37	38	39	40
41	42	43	44	45	46	47	48	49	50

1 2 3 4 5 6 7 8 9 10

SKIP COUNTING BY 3'S

Look at the picture. Trace the path of the butterfly.

Colour every third number. One has been done for you.

1	2	3	4	5	6	7	8	9	10
11	12	13	14	15	16	17	18	19	20
21	22	23	24	25	26	27	28	29	30
31	32	33	34	35	36	37	38	39	40
41	42	43	44	45	46	47	48	49	50

SKIP COUNTING BY 5'S

Look at the picture. Trace the path of the butterfly.

Colour every fifth number. One has been done for you.

1	2	3	4	5	6	7	8	9	10
11	12	13	14	15	16	17	18	19	20
21	22	23	24	25	26	27	28	29	30
31	32	33	34	35	36	37	38	39	40
41	42	43	44	45	46	47	48	49	50

1 2 3 4 5 6 7 8 9 10

SKIP COUNTING BY 10'S

Look at the picture. Trace the path of the butterfly.

1	2	3	4	5	6	7	8	9	10
11	12	13	14	15	16	17	18	19	20
21	22	23	24	25	26	27	28	29	30
31	32	33	34	35	36	37	38	39	40

Colour every tenth number. One has been done for you.

1	2	3	4	5	6	7	8	9	10
11	12	13	14	15	16	17	18	19	20
21	22	23	24	25	26	27	28	29	30
31	32	33	34	35	36	37	38	39	40
41	42	43	44	45	46	47	48	49	50

BIG AND SMALL NUMBERS

Cross out (✗) the small number in each set.

Tick (✓) the big number in each set.

BIGGEST AND SMALLEST NUMBERS

Colour the smallest number blue. One has been done for you.

34 45 41

27 50 43

16 8 39

12 47 33

Colour the biggest number green and the smallest number yellow in each set.

10 20 30 40 50

12 20 25 32 44

17 19 31 43 50

I CAN ARRANGE NUMBERS TILL 100

Write the biggest number in the red box.
Write the smallest number in the blue box.

				Red box	Blue box
12	14	16	24		
18	22	25	30		
32	22	12	2		

Write the numbers from the biggest to the smallest.
One has been done for you.

				→				
34	11	45	23	→	45	34	23	11
22	29	14	50	→				
32	48	17	9	→				

1 2 3 4 5 6 7 8 9 10

Write the numbers from the smallest to the biggest. One has been done for you.

30 12 44 50 → | 12 | 30 | 44 | 50 |

13 19 21 25 → | | | | |

50 2 34 21 → | | | | |

39 26 17 49 → | | | | |

19 28 37 46 → | | | | |

48 7 16 23 → | | | | |

BIGGEST AND SMALLEST NUMBERS

Colour the smallest number blue. One has been done for you.

29	50	81

11	90	13

10	70	56

68	46	66

Colour the biggest number green and the smallest number yellow in each set.

10	48	96	83	67

39	50	26	18	20

62	74	95	43	32

I CAN ARRANGE NUMBERS

Write the biggest number in the red box.
Write the smallest number in the blue box.

				Red box	Blue box
30	35	64	97		
12	14	11	26		
39	28	62	80		

Write the numbers from the biggest to the smallest.
One has been done for you.

				→				
24	37	52	93	→	93	52	37	24
72	28	49	60	→				
82	87	51	38	→				

Write the numbers from the smallest to the biggest. One has been done for you.

10	19	17	→	10	17	19
33	26	58	→			
29	89	43	→			
62	48	95	→			
58	72	61	→			
23	52	33	→			

NUMBER COMPARISON

8 6

>

8 > 6

5 5

=

5 = 5

6 9

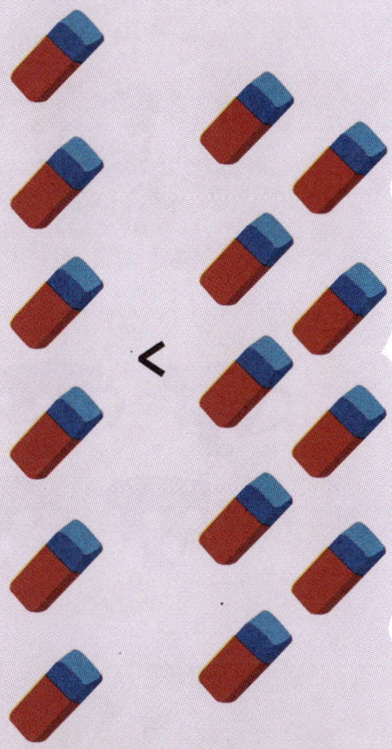

<

6 < 9

7 < 8

less than

11 > 8

greater than

3 = 3

equal to

Place the correct sign from those given <, > and =. One has been done for you.

<

 ☐ 

 ☐ 

 ☐ 

 ☐ 

NUMBER COMPARISON TILL 100

Fill in the blanks with '<' Less than, '>' Greater than or '=' Equal to.

35 ☐ 52	40 ☐ 74	45 ☐ 30
84 ☐ 77	38 ☐ 64	51 ☐ 39
43 ☐ 43	79 ☐ 28	99 ☐ 89
23 ☐ 22	66 ☐ 77	6 ☐ 16
98 ☐ 89	18 ☐ 18	30 ☐ 49

11 12 13 14 15 16 17 18 19 20

TIME

Read this poem.

I am a clock, a clock am I
I am always ticking, I never lie.
I have two arms short and long,
They move to their own song.
The long arm is thin and quick,
The short arm is slow, not sick.
Tick-tock-tick, tick-tock-tick
Time is running, I say be quick.

Clock

A clock tells us the time. A clock has two hands.

The short hand is the **hour hand**.

The long hand is the **minute hand**.

Telling the time.

In this clock, the minute hand is at 12. The hour hand is at 3. Time is 3 o'clock.

In this clock, the minute hand is at 12. The hour hand is at 7 Time is 7 o'clock.

In this clock, the minute hand is at 12. The hour hand is also at 12 Time is 12 o'clock.

Tell us where the minute and hour hands are.

Minute hand is at ____________

Hour hand is at ____________

Time is _______ o'clock

Minute hand is at ____________

Hour hand is at ____________

Time is _______ o'clock

Draw the hands on the clock that match the time in the box.

12 o'clock

7 o'clock

11 o'clock

2 o'clock

10 o'clock

8 o'clock

1 o'clock

3 o'clock

6 o'clock

NUMBER BONDS

Count and write the number of blue dots.

10
5

10
6

10
7

10
8

10
9

NUMBER BONDS

Draw the correct number of red dots.
One has been done for you.

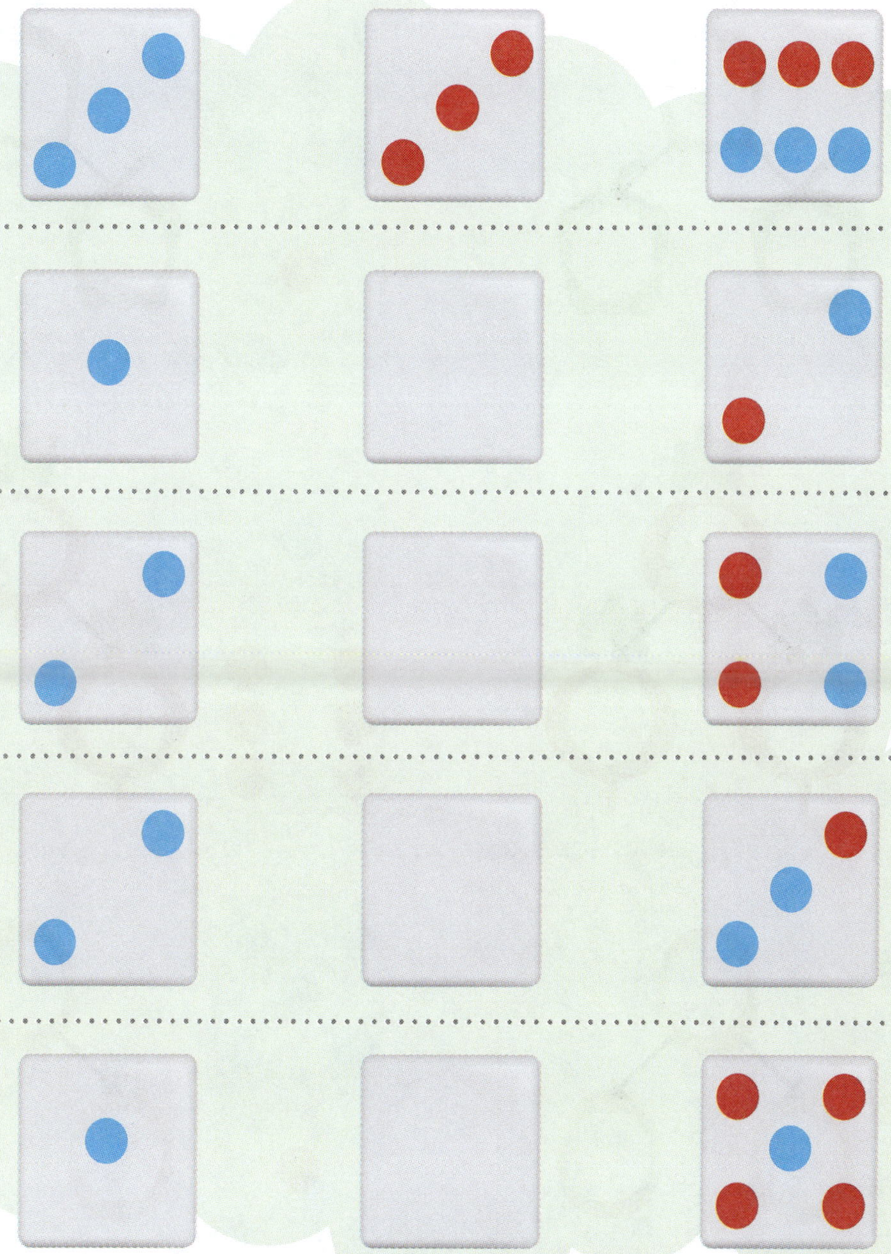

Fill in the missing numbers. One has been done for you.

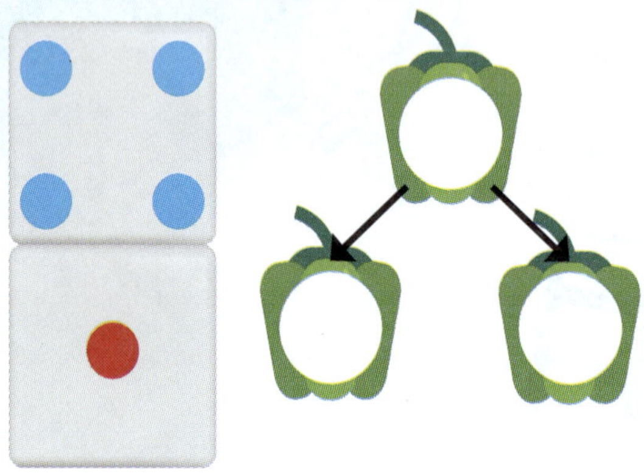

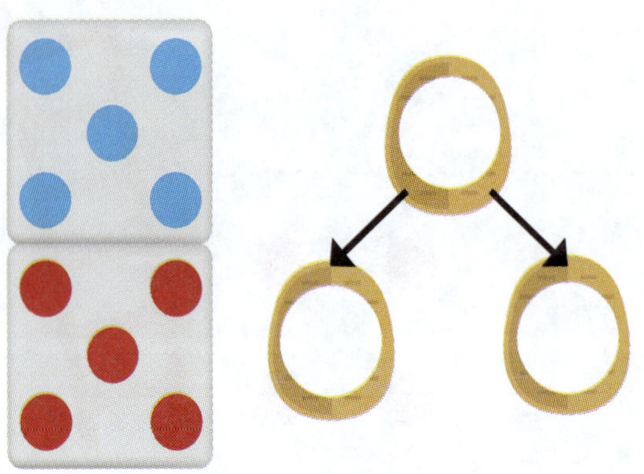

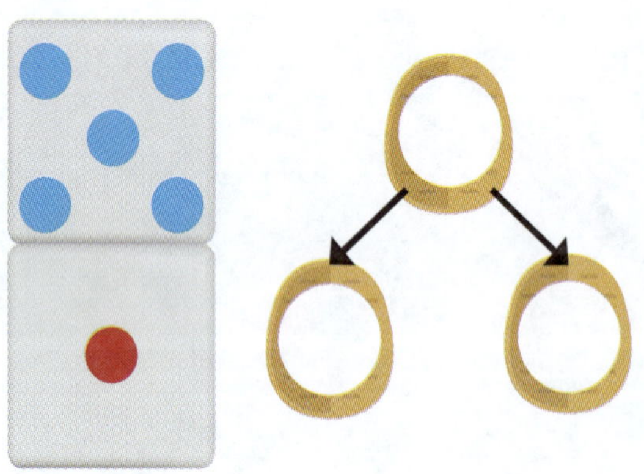

DANCING BUTTERFLIES

Sing.

One butterfly with nothing to do
Along came I more and now there are two.

Two little butterflies flying free.
Along came I more and now there are three.

Three little butterflies flying high and low
Along came I more and now there are four.

Four little butterflies touching the sky
Along came I more and now there are five.

Five little butterflies play in the garden,
Singing in the rain, dancing in the sun.

Draw 1 more object. Count and write the total number.

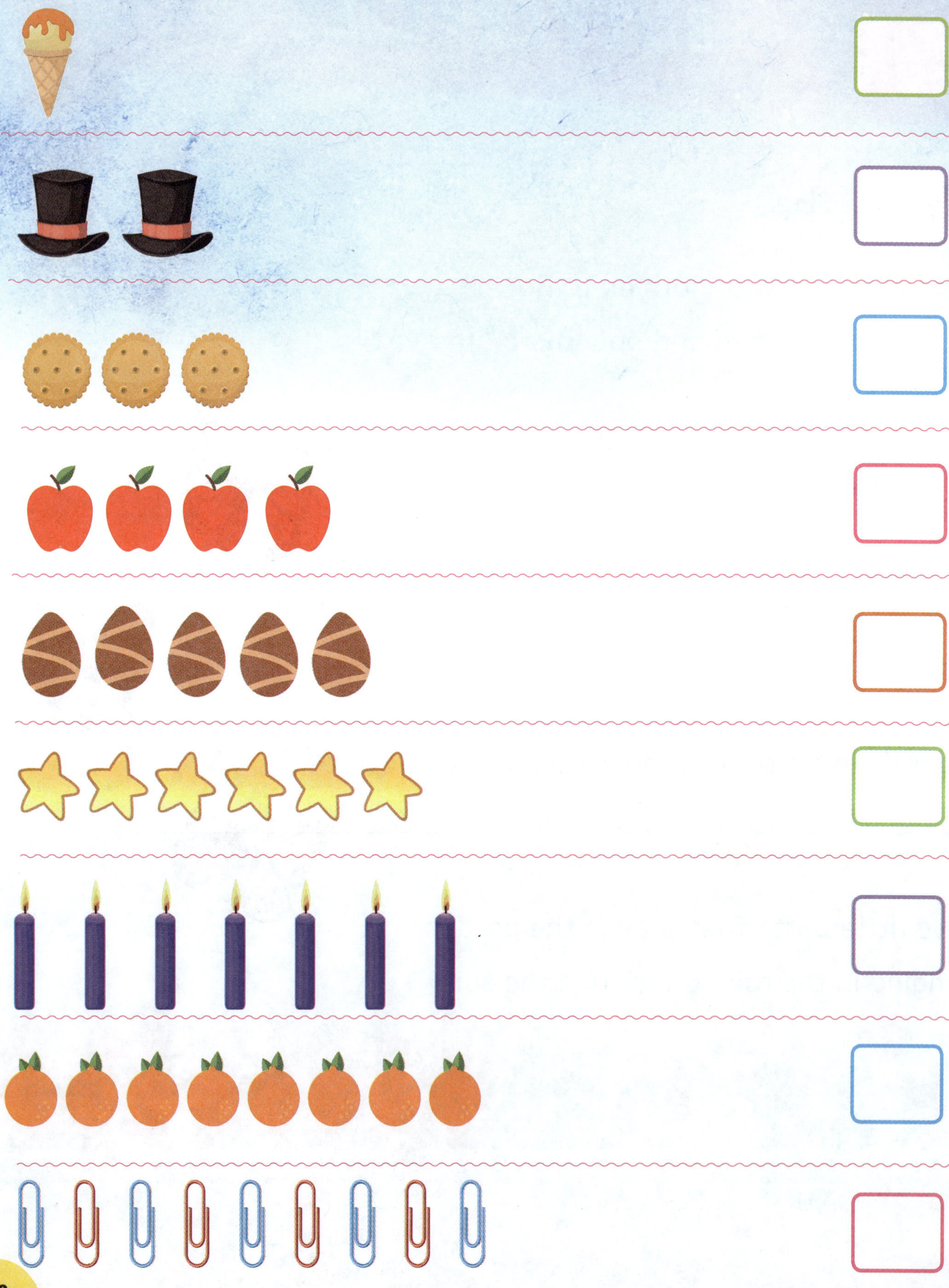

1 2 3 4 5 6 7 8 9 10

ADDITION

Count and draw. One has been done for you.

 and  make 

 and  make

 and  make

 and  make

 and  make

 and  make

Count and add. One has been done for you.

'+' means to add

$$\begin{array}{r} 2 \\ +\ 2 \\ \hline 4 \end{array}$$

2 and 2 make <u>4</u>

We can write this as (2 + 2 = <u>4</u>)

It is read as 2 plus 2 equals 4.

$$\begin{array}{r} 2 \\ +\ 4 \\ \hline \end{array}$$

$$\begin{array}{r} 3 \\ +\ 3 \\ \hline \end{array}$$

$$\begin{array}{r} 5 \\ +\ 4 \\ \hline \end{array}$$

$$\begin{array}{r} 4 \\ +\ 3 \\ \hline \end{array}$$

1 2 3 4 5 6 7 8 9 10

PICTURE ADDITION

Count and write.

 and  make 7

☐ ☐

 and  make 5

☐ ☐

Count and add.

1 + 3 = ☐

5 + 1 = ☐

NUMBER LINE ADDITION

Use the number line to help solve.

5 + 2 = ☐

3 + 4 = ☐

2 + 7 = ☐

8 + 1 = ☐

ADDITION STORIES

There are 5 bees playing in a park. 3 more bees join them.
How many bees are playing in the park now? ☐

4 swans are playing in a pond. 3 more swans join them.
How many swans are there in all? ☐

11 12 13 14 15 16 17 18 19 20

FIVE LITTLE CHICKS

Sing.

5 little chicks inside 5 eggs,
All of them peck away at the shells.
Out comes 1 and flies away,
4 little chicks still peck away.

4 little chicks inside 4 eggs,
All of them peck away at the shells.
Out comes 1 and flies away,
3 little chicks still peck away.

Continue the rhyme with 3 chicks and 2 chicks, till 1 chick is left.

1 little chick inside 1 egg,
All it does is peck away at the shells.
Out it comes and flies away,
All the chicks fly through the day.

Cross out (✗) 1 object. Count and write the total number.

11 12 13 14 15 16 17 18 19 20

SUBTRACTION

Cross out (✗). Count and draw. One has been done for you.

'–' means to remove or take away

There are 9 balls.
6 balls are taken away.
Now there are 3 balls left.
We can write these as 9 – 6 = 3

5 - 3 = ☐

6 - 4 = ☐

8 - 7 = ☐

5 - 2 = ☐

1 2 3 4 5 6 7 8 9 10

Cross out (✗), count and write. One has been done for you.

6
− 2
4

5
− 3

4
− 1

7
− 4

9
− 5

7
− 6

SUBTRACTION STORIES

1. Mary has 6 cherries. She eats 2 of them. How many cherries are left?

☐ – ☐ = ☐

2. There are 8 orange slices in a plate. Pam eats 3 of them. How many orange slices are there in the plate now?

☐ – ☐ = ☐

3. Tina has 5 candies. She gave 4 of them to Rosy. How many candies are left with Tina?

☐ – ☐ = ☐

1 2 3 4 5 6 7 8 9 10

I KNOW ADDITION AND SUBTRACTION

Count, draw and write.

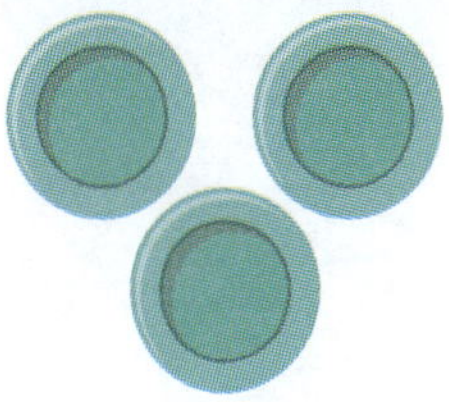 and 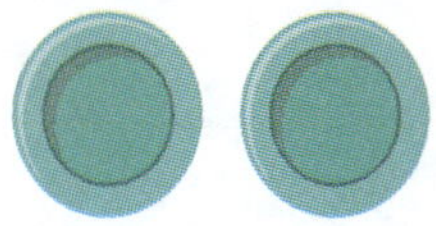 = ☐

 and  = ☐

 and  = ☐

 and  = ☐

 and  = ☐

Count, cross out and write the correct number.

5 – 2 = ☐

4 – 3 = ☐

6 – 4 = ☐

7 – 3 = ☐

MONEY

We need money to buy things.
Look at the money we use.

5 rupees ₹5

10 rupees ₹10

20 rupees ₹20

50 rupees ₹50

100 rupees ₹100

200 rupees ₹200

Counting ₹ coins

one-rupee coin

five-rupee coin

two-rupee coin

ten-rupee coin

Let's go Shopping!

Draw a line from the ice cream to the money you need to buy it.

See the amount of the item and write the remaining change to be taken from the shop vendor.

Price of the item	Amount paid	Change to be given
₹5 		₹
₹15 	 	₹
₹10 		₹
₹8 		₹
₹15 		₹

COUNTING FROM 101 TO 110

Trace and write.

101	101		106	106	
102	102		107	107	
103	103		108	108	
104	104		109	109	
105	105		110	110	

COUNTING FROM 111 TO 120

Trace and write.

111	111		116	116	
112	112		117	117	
113	113		118	118	
114	114		119	119	
115	115		120	120	

COUNTING FROM 121 TO 130

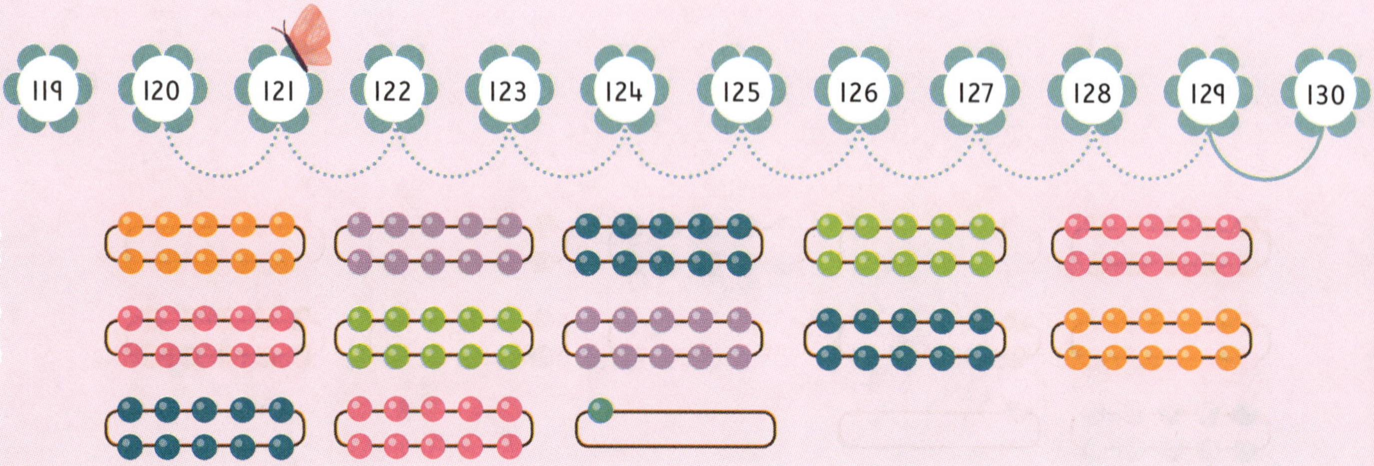

Trace and write.

121	121		126	126	
122	122		127	127	
123	123		128	128	
124	124		129	129	
125	125		130	130	

COUNTING FROM 131 TO 140

Trace and write.

131	131		136	136	
132	132		137	137	
133	133		138	138	
134	134		139	139	
135	135		140	140	

COUNTING FROM 141 TO 150

Trace and write.

141	141		146	146	
142	142		147	147	
143	143		148	148	
144	144		149	149	
145	145		150	150	

I KNOW COUNTING FROM 101 TO 150

Fill in the missing numbers.

101	111		131	
102				
103				
				144
	115			145
106				
				147
108	118			148
		129		
				150

I KNOW NUMBERS FROM 101 to 150

Match the pictures to the correct numbers.

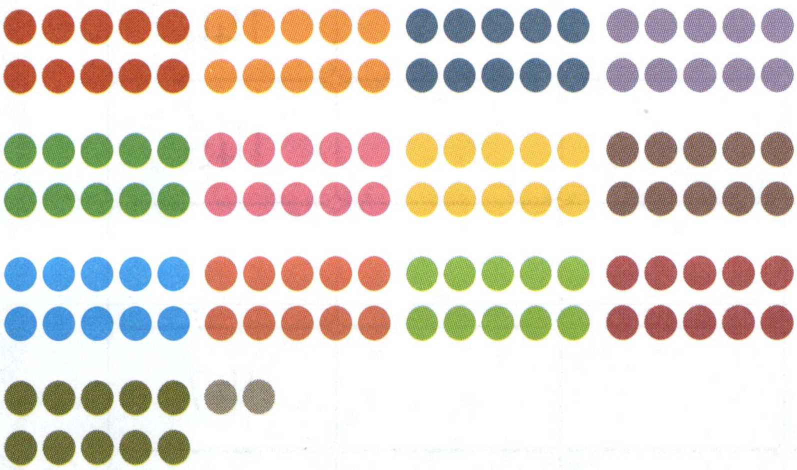

125

142

132

NUMBERS TILL 150: MORE – LESS

Cross out (✗) the one that is more.

Colour the number that comes before.

132 133 145 146

122 123

Cross out (✗) the number that comes after.

126 127 139 140

148 149

Ring the number that comes in between.

109 110 111 140 141 142

132 133 134

COUNTING FROM 151 TO 160

149 150 151 152 153 154 155 156 157 158 159 160

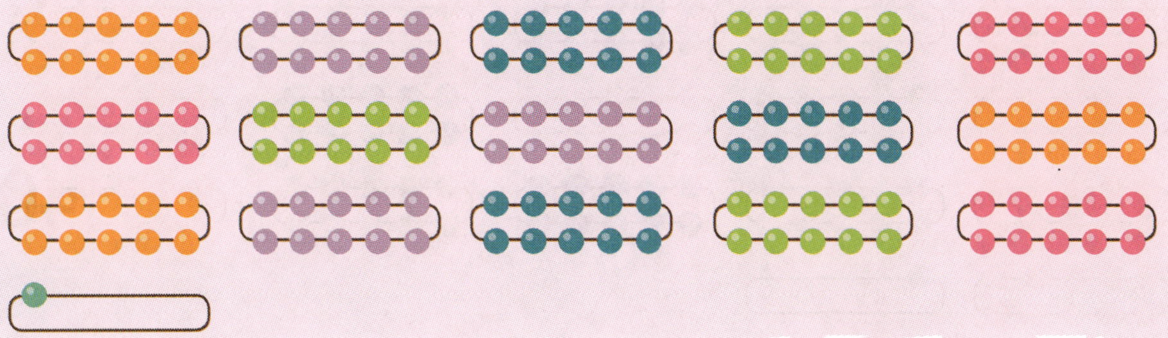

Trace and write.

151	151		156	156	
152	152		157	157	
153	153		158	158	
154	154		159	159	
155	155		160	160	

COUNTING FROM 161 TO 170

159 160 161 162 163 164 165 166 167 168 169 170

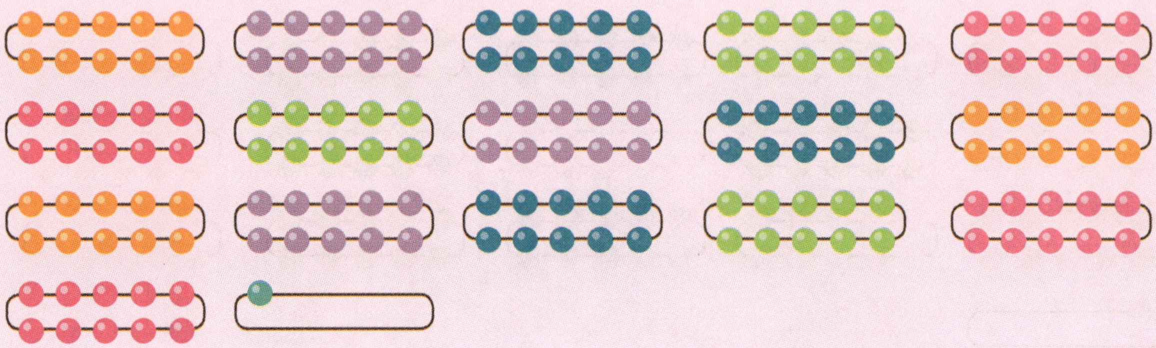

Trace and write.

161	161		166	166	
162	162		167	167	
163	163		168	168	
164	164		169	169	
165	165		170	170	

COUNTING FROM 171 TO 180

169 170 171 172 173 174 175 176 177 178 179 180

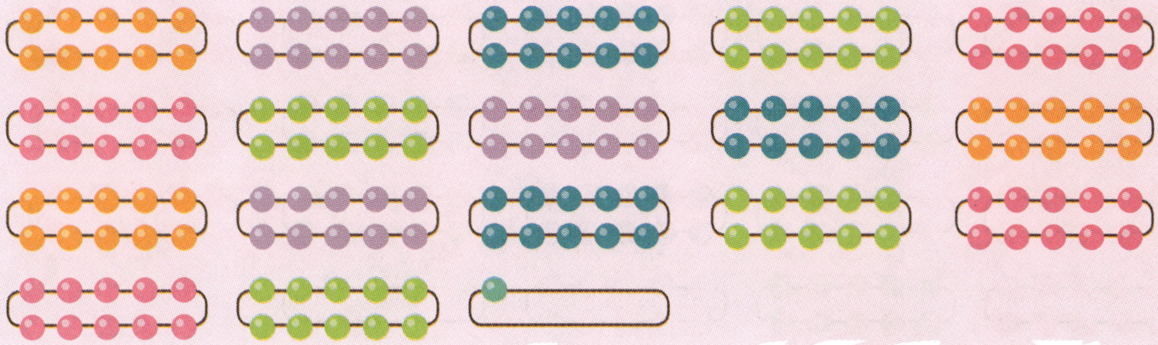

Trace and write.

171	171		176	176	
172	172		177	177	
173	173		178	178	
174	174		179	179	
175	175		180	180	

COUNTING FROM 181 TO 190

179 180 181 182 183 184 185 186 187 188 189 190

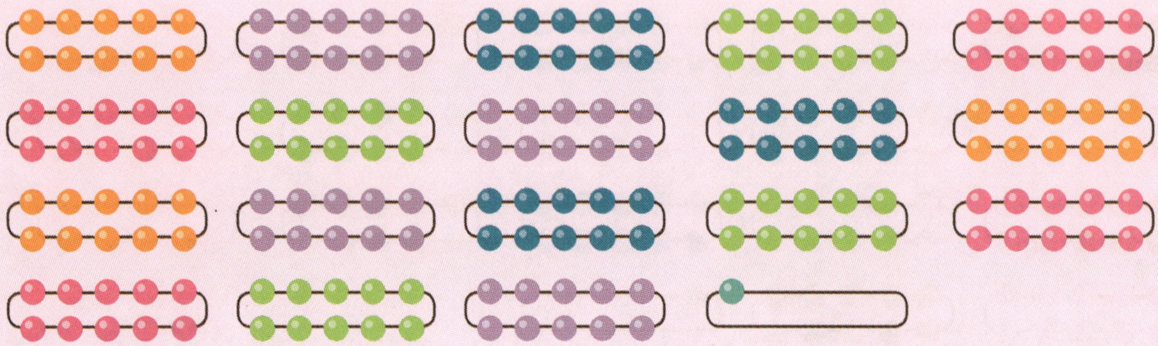

Trace and write.

181	181		186	186	
182	182		187	187	
183	183		188	188	
184	184		189	189	
185	185		190	190	

COUNTING FROM 191 TO 200

Trace and write.

191	191		196	196	
192	192		197	197	
193	193		198	198	
194	194		199	199	
195	195		200	200	

I KNOW NUMBERS FROM 151 TO 200

Write the numbers that come just before.

___ 172   ___ 184   ___ 177   ___ 195

Write the numbers that come just after.

181 ___   165 ___   198 ___   162 ___

Write the missing number between the given numbers.

164 ___ 166   172 ___ 174

187 ___ 189   153 ___ 155

Match the pictures to the correct numbers.

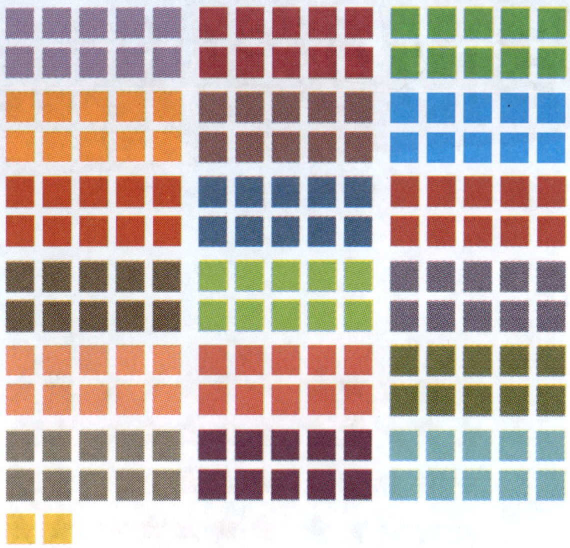

182

194

175

NUMBERS TILL 200: MORE-LESS

Cross out (✗) the one that is more.

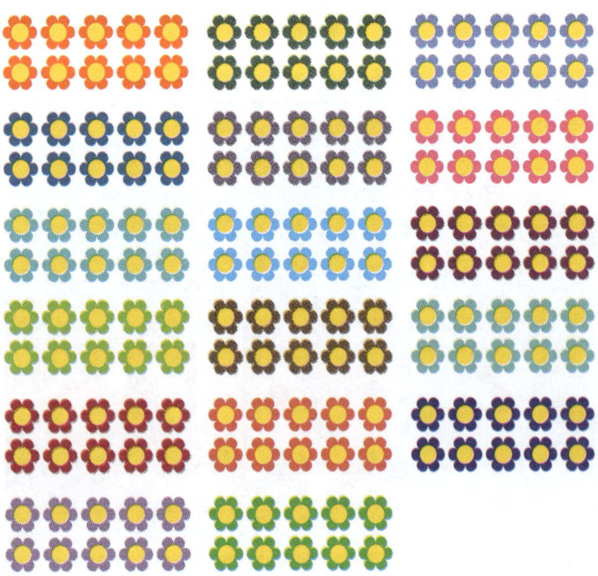

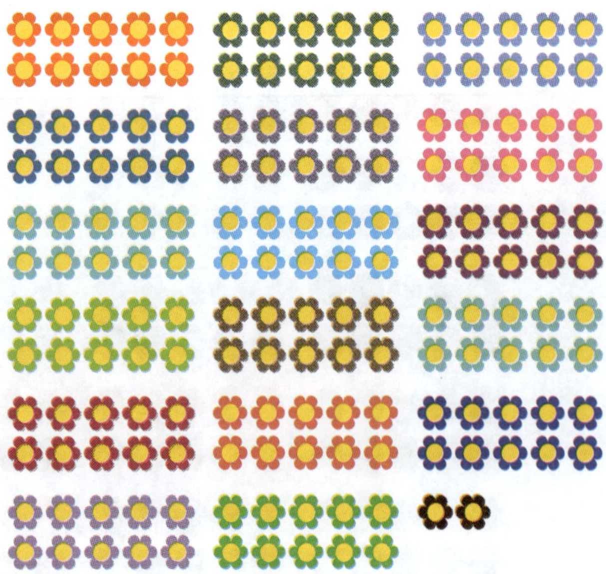